# GET OUT OF
# MY HEAD!

# GET OUT OF MY HEAD!

## My Life With OCD

ALISON ISLIN
&
JUDY KARBRITZ

**Poetry Press Ltd**

# GET OUT OF MY HEAD!

ALISON ISLIN & JUDY KARBRITZ

First Published in 2006 by

Poetry Press Ltd
26 Park Grove, Edgware, Middx, HA8 7SJ

ISBN 0-9548596-6-9

*My doctor said I had OCD.*
*I couldn't believe it.*
*I had to call him nine times to make sure.*

*Judy Gold*

# ACKNOWLEDGEMENTS

I want to thank Judy for giving me an opportunity to reach out to a wider audience, and for her constant and continued support both as a co-author and a very dear friend. My thanks and gratitude go unreservedly to Dr David Veale and Rob Wilson for helping me enjoy my life, and for enriching it in the process.

Of course it goes without saying how absolutely huge my gratitude is to all at Barnet Voice, because without the constant, unprejudiced friendship we give to one another my state of mind would not be as good as it is now. A massive thanks to Elsie Lyons, my boss and mentor. Thank you too, Suzanne, for introducing me to Barnet Voice, and in doing so creating the opportunity for my career in mental health to flourish.

A big thank you to Mum and Dad for their endless love and support and to my lovely brother Dr Stephen Malnick, my wonderful sister-in-law Aliza and my nephew and two nieces.

My list of thank-yous would not be complete without my darling Brian who has given me unstinting support, kindness and stability over the last 23 years of our joint lives. He is truly my better half. And, finally, to Mark and Mitchell, whom I adore unconditionally and love more than is possible to say. I am so proud of you both.

In other words, I dedicate this book to:

The Three Men In My Life
Brian, Mark and Mitchell
*and Woody*

Alison Islin

# Judy Karbritz

My awareness of OCD began several years ago when I worked on a helpline for adult survivors of childhood abuse. Over the telephone I got to know a lady who was crippled by OCD as a result of being abused by her father.

She neither bathed nor brushed her teeth because, as she explained to me, although a "normal" person would take ten minutes to have a bath, it would take her several hours and if she was interrupted or forgot how many times she had rubbed the soap then she had to start again. Brushing her teeth also was a Herculean task, which she no longer had the strength to accomplish.

She dearly wanted to write to me but couldn't trust herself not to write an obscenity on the envelope, no matter how many times she reread it. OCD isn't called The Doubting Disease for nothing.

This was my first introduction to OCD and I wanted to find out more. I was introduced to Suzanne who assisted Alison at her OCD Support Group at The Priory and she kindly invited me to attend a meeting.

Alison and I hit it off straight away. She's a loving, sensitive, generous, self-deprecating woman who flings herself wholeheartedly into life – her enthusiasm for writing her story has been as infectious as a dry cough at the theatre.

Suzanne and I now run an OCD Support Group and I actually have a chocolate cake in the oven while I write this as next week our group celebrates our fifth anniversary.

Alison and I met most weeks for lunch while we worked on the book. In fact, this is the only book I know which, instead of being calculated by the amount of words or pages, has been estimated by the number of smoked salmon bagels and fish balls consumed.

Joking apart, Alison has given a brutally honest, often ugly and searingly painful look at what it feels like to live with OCD. But, like all the best stories, this one also ends on an uplifting note as Alison has finally reclaimed her life.

The purpose of writing *Get Out Of My Head!* was to help those of you who suffer with OCD to believe that you really can get through the blackest days, and for it also to be an anchor for those readers who have family or friends who suffer from OCD. Not forgetting those who simply want a jolly good read about a condition that is attracting a great deal of media attention.

There are so many people who have helped me whilst writing this book and I thank you all. I must give special thanks, though, to the American artist Maggie Blue for her cover design, Helen Schifreen for proof reading and my daughter, Karen Yarris, for her invaluable help and support.

www.judyk.co.uk

# CONTENTS

# FOREWORD

Obsessive Compulsive Disorder can blight lives. It is in the Top Ten of the World Health Organisations' list of disorders that cause the most impairment of life. The effects of OCD ripple to impact on the partner, family, friends, employers and society.

What's more, it takes on average about seven years for a person with OCD to get a diagnosis. There may then be further hoops for a sufferer for being on a waiting list for treatment or being given ineffective treatments.

Alison movingly describes her experience with OCD and depression, her distress and disability. The story is also one of hope as she demonstrates that it is possible to stand up to the bully that is OCD. This was despite being offered inappropriate treatment, from which she was able to escape. We learn how she recognizes that her solutions were her problems, and that what she thought was her friend was her enemy.

Once Alison started to overcome her OCD, she was able to follow her valued directions in life by being a better partner and parent. She developed a new role in life in facilitating an OCD and Barnet Voice support group. In this regard, I think she deserves an honour. I am personally grateful both for the voluntary work that Alison has done for the OCD support group at The Priory North London and for the many sufferers and families that she has helped over the years.

In reading her book I have also learnt much from Alison even if it does describe events that occurred some fourteen years ago as our practice and service has developed.

This book will, I hope, help anyone who suffers from OCD and their carers. I hope it will help to increase awareness of OCD, and get across the message that OCD can be treated and it is possible to get your life back.

DAVID VEALE
Consultant Psychiatrist
in Cognitive Behaviour Therapy
The South London and Maudsley Trust and
The Priory Hospital North London
www.veale.co.uk

# A HOLIDAY FROM MY MIND

They lurk in gloomy shadows deep
Long days and nights they haunt me
On constant guard, not needing sleep
They wait to pounce and taunt me
They censor everything I say
I can't leave them behind
Wish I could take a holiday
And travel from my mind

They put ideas into my head
That echo round and round
I try to drown them out instead
My temples throb and pound
I see the world in black and grey
No colours left to find
Wish I could take a holiday
And travel from my mind

Contaminating all I touch
My hands are clothed in dirt
I scrub them but it's not enough
Yet still they bleed and hurt
I beg that they might go away
Though fear we're intertwined
Wish I could take a holiday
And travel from my mind

I've broken keys through checking locks
I can't trust what I see
I'm plagued by doubts, it never stops
They mock me constantly
Am I so wicked I can't pray?
But surely God is kind
Wish I could take a holiday
And travel from my mind

©2006 Judy Karbritz

# Chapter 1
# ROOM 13

*Everything else you grow out of,*
*but you never recover from childhood*
*Beryl Bainbridge*

We called it Dracula's Drive. The road down to
The Priory was wide and winding with occasional
speed humps rising like giant molehills in a plush,
newly mown lawn. At night, the branches of the trees
and bushes that grew either side took the form of
spindly touching fingers that blocked out any
moonlight.

I was huddled miserably in the back of my
husband Brian's car one freezing morning in January
1993. I was 32, a mass of obsessions, compulsions
and nerves. My skin was raw from where I'd picked
it, my eyebrows virtually non-existent from constantly
pulling at them. All this took place in public; when I
was alone I tore out my pubic hairs to get some relief
from a devil I was about to face, here at The Priory.

As you will discover, my journey to The Priory
was far longer and more tortuous than that seemingly
endless half mile down Dracula's Drive.

Like a rabid dog finally too exhausted to drag
wildly at its chain but now lying slumped on the
ground, I too had reached the end of my tether. I had
no more fight left and finally admitted that I needed

help. I had confronted what I was, and no longer kidded myself that I was normal.

And now I was being voluntarily admitted into this sanctuary in the hope that I could learn to live and function as any other normal woman.

What was normal? To me it was a woman in her 30's who could clean her teeth, remove the day's make-up and empty a dishwasher. It isn't that I didn't want to do any of these ordinary daily activities. I desperately wanted to do them but I simply couldn't.

I felt I was in an ever-decreasing spiral, being sucked into a black hole by my fears, obsessions and compulsions. By now it was affecting all my family in ways you wouldn't immediately imagine. "Mummy washes her hands over and over till they bleed and has to make breakfast in a certain order."

I had to dress my children in a certain way, left sock then right sock. Left leg went into trousers first and left arm had to go into sleeves before the right. If they did it in the wrong order or if my concentration was broken we had to start all over again.

I would make a drink before the cereal or toast. When I buttered the toast I had to wipe the vestiges of butter off the knife so that I could see the serrated edge.

Although, as you will discover, I have come so far since those days I still have a need to carefully wipe my knife as well as having to arrange the plates in order of my children's age. They say old age isn't for cissies; in my opinion neither is OCD.

Even though I couldn't have done it for myself, most mothers will know the feeling of superhuman strength when it comes to protecting their children. This maternal force made me stronger as I couldn't let my children be victims of my demon any longer.

14

Protecting them with my life would have been simple compared with this. I was determined to claw back my health, my mental health and, God help me, I was going to control OCD and become the mother my boys deserved.

I'd reached out for a haven and Dr Veale, my psychiatrist, provided the lifeboat, but I knew it was up to me to sail it to dry land. He may have rescued me but in the end it was down to me to save myself.

Dr Veale was aware that I could only function if I used the crutch of relying on my superstitions. I avoided doing anything that meant an odd number. This affected me in so many ways; for instance, from how many lamp posts I walked past or the number of days I went on holiday to even the amount of peanuts I ate.

Why did I do it? I felt uncomfortable if I didn't and that caused anxiety. Don't ask me why, it simply was the case. The trouble was that avoidance only made it worse and the only way to get used to it was through exposure.

So, no believer in pussyfooting around, Dr Veale insisted I stay in Room 13. I told myself that if I wanted to get better I had to endure anything he threw at me and if Room 13 was part of the treatment then so be it.

When I entered my room I was pleasantly surprised. The room was quite big, dominated by a single bed. It had one armchair and curtains and bedspread that all co-ordinated. I had a dresser-come-desk with a mirror, and a lovely long window with only a small opening from the bottom. Then I saw it for the first time; pictures on the walls had no glass in them. The television was stuck down. There were no locks to my bedroom door or - worse - to my ensuite bathroom.

A nurse examined my luggage to see I had nothing there with which I could harm myself. She checked to see I had no laces in my shoes, or even make-up sharpeners with blades.

As it happens this wasn't necessary, because I have never self-harmed, at least not with knives, blades or laces. Most of my OCD centred around contamination.

I know you may think I've glossed over the skin picking and hair pulling, which is a form of self-harm but not quite the same as cutting yourself and gaining release in seeing the blood pour.

There were, however, incidents of injury. The only way I could be sure, for instance, that the bath was clean was to hurt myself by banging my hand on the wall. One day I cut my finger on a broken tile, and remember being spellbound as the blood made patterns on the white porcelain.

But now it was time for lunch; my first meal at The Priory. I had already asked Dr Veale if I could take all my meals in room 13, but I was firmly told that I must join in with the other residents and learn how to socialise here at meal times. But why should I? After all, I wasn't one of them was I? These people weren't like me; they were going to be mental and, disturbed as I was, surely I wasn't mad.

I forced myself to walk into the dining room and my eyes immediately went to Bob, a good-looking guy with almost shoulder length hair, sitting at a corner table by the large patio windows. In a small voice I asked if I could sit down and another man sat down too. I felt so nervous for I believed that a mental health patient was indeed barmy.

We started to make some small talk, that came to an abrupt end when Bob announced, "I am not a frog".

16

Charlie, the other man on our table, ignored us and stared at his plate, eating as though he were a robot. He dripped a little bright red bolognaise sauce on his chin and Bob, in his American drawl, accused him, "You're a slob". But he could have been addressing the plate of spaghetti for the attention Charlie paid him.

Bob wasn't the only character here in North London's top clinic. Peter, a drug addict, discovered a talent for pottery while having occupational therapy. I remember one particular piece he made, a sculpture of a skull. As far as I could tell, it was absolutely perfectly crafted. But what made it so memorably shocking was that it had an axe embedded in it. I asked him why, and he told me his father had hit him over the head with an axe.

Cissie, a talented artist, had painted a picture of New York. The left side had the sun shining and it was a beautiful day with trees, flowers and children all in vibrant colours; the other side depicted a storm with lightning flashing, and blood dripping down the sides of the buildings.

But now I was being ushered back to my room. As the nurse left the room it was as though a light switch had been turned off. Unwanted thoughts, which to most people would be unwelcome but not all consuming, flooded my mind. But to someone whose mind was already tormented by illogical fears, these intrusive thoughts or ruminations were too powerful to control. "Will I be murdered during the night as I sleep?" "Would I be drowned in the bath?" I sat on the bed, clenching my fists until my nails drew blood as I felt my heart beat faster and my body trembled as I waited alone in Room 13.

## Chapter 2
## THE JULIE GAME

*Nobody can make you feel inferior*
*without your consent*
*Eleanor Roosevelt*

I have often wondered what it feels like actually to be happy. Certainly no one has ever been able to tell me, yet that would be the only way I would know because I am pretty certain I have never experienced it. I am not talking about laughing with friends, or a blissful or passionate night. I am talking about contentment.

Certainly schooldays, those days that are often referred to as the happiest in your life, were far from that for me.

The bullying must have started when I was seven or eight. I was one of the few Jewish children in the school, my older brother being another, and rather than stamp collecting, hair braiding or skipping, the most popular pastime was Jew-baiting. Anti-Semitism was rife.

There were three of us Jewish girls in my year. The other two girls were timid and did their best to avoid the bullies who'd pull our hair and call us names. Not me though, oh no, I refused to run and hide. Instead, I answered them back – and how I eventually suffered for it.

When I was in infant school, my proudest moment came when I was picked to take the two school gerbils home for the weekend. I felt like a princess when my name was read out.

Friday afternoon, my mother collected me from school. I told the gerbils that they were going to go on holiday and carefully emptied their water bowl. Together, Mum and I carried Pixie and Dixie along with all their paraphernalia.

Have you ever heard the fairy story about Princess Alison? I'm not surprised you haven't as it was a very short story. It lasted until we left the school and then Alison was a princess no longer.

There must have been about ten young thugs running parallel to us on the opposite side of the road. Not only had they no respect for me, they had scant regard for my mother either. "Can't touch those f-ing gerbils again, they're contaminated with Jew dirt" they taunted.

Nothing stopped them. We walked faster until we were almost what today would be considered jogging. Yet the faster we ran, the faster they ran and the louder they shouted. My mother was more shaken than she let me know.

The pleasure had now gone from taking care of Pixie and Dixie. Every time I fed them or talked to them that weekend, the jeers reverberated in my head and I shut my eyes very tightly to try to stop it, but nothing helped. Nothing, that is, except my doll Julie.

My naked doll, Julie, was indeed my only comfort. For hours at a time I played my "Julie Game". This meant I talked to her, nursed her and knew that she depended on me. I felt I didn't have another friend in the world, and best of all, Julie needed me.

The bullying got worse each term. I was locked in the school toilets and had pins stuck in my bottom until blood pierced my skin, staining my knickers.

My lunch-box was repeatedly kicked around the playground like a football, and I was endlessly kicked, punched and slapped.

Looking back, it's hardly surprising that I began to develop Obsessive Compulsive Disorder.

It came gradually. At first I picked at my skin while I stayed in my bedroom whispering to myself.

Each morning as I woke, rather like a serial dieter every Monday, I would tell myself "right, now my life begins". I'd spend four or five hours at a time locked in the garage.

I started off by talking to an imaginary audience but actually spoke to Julie. I would introduce my name in full "Alison Dianne Sharon Malnick", and then on my list I introduced all my family, mentioning the men first with a little résumé.

I then gave a potted biography. I talked about what happened in school, my operations and who'd upset me.

For those few hours it was like a rebirth, and I believed that my life would be different afterwards but it never was; it was far more a hamster wheel of catharsis.

This was the Julie game, which I played over and over. I talked out loud, laughed and cried, no holds barred as I spoke about every fear, hope, and resolution that haunted me.

It wasn't a phase, this huge splurge of my time.

*Alison and her Julie doll*

It was a regular occurrence until I was 21 and met my husband. It was only then that this incessant need to "bring everything outside my head" at last faded as he filled that space within me.

It should have been the happiest time of my life. This other part of me, the miserable little girl who only had a doll to love should have disappeared but instead she was still there.

This is when the obsessions began. I felt they were my way of controlling fate and keeping a grip. I had to wash myself in a certain order, walked in a particular way and was unable to do housework if I didn't like the date. It got worse, because if I read that someone had died I had to write off the entire day.

Little by little, the obsessions began to control me and like any untamed beast they demanded nourishment. The only way I kept them at bay was to placate them with compulsions.

As with any plague it was swift and all consuming, and there was to be no respite.

# Chapter 3
# OCD – THE BEGINNINGS

*Life can only be understood backwards;*
*but it must be lived forwards*
*Soren Kierkegaard*

I think I can understand how Alice felt when she followed the White Rabbit and began her adventures in Wonderland. She had no control of the madness around her, yet strived to make sense of this strange new world.

In a bizarre way, when I was at primary school I came to believe that the insanity began and ended with me. Had the other children simply ignored me then I could have coped. I often cried myself to sleep praying that I would be ignored. But bullying is far more menacing; it creeps into your bones and I knew that if I were to keep my sanity I had to claim some sort of power back.

I could only control myself, my body. And I was going to be mistress of it, make it do what I wanted when I wanted. However, Alice was no longer in Wonderland but had passed into the topsy-turvy world of the Looking Glass as my mind and then my body began to control me. I'd begun with tapping my right foot before I went into bed. No big deal you may think, but it gathered in momentum when I had to check the clock didn't show a time that made me feel uncomfortable. What was it that made me uncomfortable? It was certain numbers and combinations of numbers. Yes, I may have created all these compulsions, but like Frankenstein's monster their power took on a strength of its own.

Washing my hair, my hands and myself had to be executed to a set routine. And do you know the maddest part of it? This folly kept me sane.

All this time, I felt I was on my own without even my parents to protect me. In my final year of primary school they agreed that the headmaster had done nothing to safeguard me. As most of the roughest of my year were going to the local secondary school my parents wanted me to be privately educated.

Looking back, it is hard to believe my naivety at the relief I felt when I was accepted into Peterborough & St Margaret's for Girls. I believed that dark place in my head was going to have the curtains drawn, and a little light would shine in. How was I to know the curtains would be exchanged for blackout shutters?

So here I was at my new school. Picture me in my uniform, all brown right down to my Bridget Jones knickers. Long beige socks and, the *pièce de résistance,* my brown felt hat, turned up and with a red ribbon, culminating in a stitched-together bow, running all around the rim.

This little girl, walking so proudly along the pavement, didn't stay proud for very long. You see, absolutely nothing had changed. The bullies lived locally and I was still their victim. Each morning they'd pull off my hat and bounce it along the pavement, kicking, punching and pummelling me.

*Alison with her parents and her brother, Stephen*

Even when my father walked me to the bus stop he was targeted with their verbal abuse and racist taunts. After school was no better, as I tried to rush home before they caught me.

By the time I was 13 the depression really kicked in. Teenagers are pretty much walking hormones at the best of times and I became lethargic with little motivation and even less self-esteem. The only constant in my life was my OCD and I turned to it rather like one would turn to a friend, a presence that's always there. I began to write weekly articles for my local newspaper *The Harrow Observer* centring on my feelings of inadequacy and fear.

The other girls at school read them and started to whisper when I came near. They thought I was weird, not only for thinking and feeling what I did, but for letting others into my world. But I was calling out in the only way I could, through the written word.

I was begging someone, anyone, to read what I'd written and reassure me that everything would be all right. And how it hurt to realize that no one was there to make it all better. Even my parents looked away from my pain and, rather like putting a toddler in pretty clothes to show off to the neighbours, my father said, "Why don't you write something a little more cheerful?"

From tapping my feet and having to wash myself in a particular way, I then developed twitches and I started to limp, enough for people to ask Mum what was wrong with my leg. I avoided certain pavement slabs if they had marks on them or were a shade I felt uncomfortable with.

My bedroom began to look like it belonged to a Stepford teenager, clean and orderly with not a lipstick out of place. Little by little, my mind overtook the external bullies, and gained complete control.

It became worse when I was 14. I discovered that I had been conceived as a twin but right at the beginning of the pregnancy my mother miscarried. She was told not to have intercourse again for the next six weeks. When she went back for her check-up she discovered she was still pregnant, pregnant with me. Coupled with my illogical compulsions, I now felt guilty for surviving whilst my twin had died. Had I taken all the nourishment from this baby or positioned myself in such a way that I thrived whilst my twin starved? My ruminations added to my obsessional thoughts, which made my compulsions spiral out of control.

My older brother Stephen was not aware of what was happening to me. He had achieved excellent A-levels and had gained a place to study medicine at Oxford University. I was so proud and was thrilled for him. Far from ever feeling jealous, I was amazed that someone related so closely to me could accomplish so much.

However, my positive feelings didn't last too long as they soon metamorphosed into overwhelming guilt. I believed it was my responsibility to keep him safe and the only way I knew how was to ritualise in order that he could remain so. This stayed with me for years and I used to pray that, rather than anything happen to him, my life should be taken as his was far more precious than mine.

# Chapter 4
# GROWING PAINS

*Life shrinks and expands*
*in proportion to one's courage*
*Anais Nin*

From my days of writing for *The Harrow Observer*, I knew I wanted to work in journalism.

As with other tens of thousands of hopefuls, I had chosen a career that was nigh impossible to get into but I was passionate about writing and tried any way I could to get an interview.

Books packed with advice on interview techniques have been written and certainly they're no picnic for anyone. I think though that I found them even more traumatic than many job hunters because I had the added burden of blame. If I didn't meet the requirements for a certain position then I placed a mountain of guilt on my shoulders and felt completely demoralised. In those days I was a mental masochist.

My first interview came about through a particularly devious route. A few years earlier, when I was fourteen, my parents took me to Cannes in the French Riviera.

We went every year for two weeks and stayed in one of the hotels in a side street near the beach. I can still remember sipping hot chocolate in the lounge of The Carlton Hotel most evenings. Bliss!

But this year was different as it was the first time my brother didn't come with us as he was on his gap year in the States before beginning university.

So that is how it came about that Mum, Dad and I did our usual sunbathing and strolling along the beachfront and ended up in The Carlton with our customary hot chocolate. I didn't feel like accompanying Mum and Dad for their evening stroll though and stayed behind in the lounge, nursing my drink.

As though he had been watching us, soon after my parents left a handsome man in his twenties sat next to me and told me he was a guest staying at the hotel.

I felt flattered that an older man showed an interest in me and agreed when he suggested we went for a walk. Within a couple of days, much to my parents' dismay, we became inappropriately close. He showered me with compliments and made me feel attractive and desirable blocking out all thoughts of OCD.

And then, as though my euphoria were a house of cards painstakingly erected only to be demolished by a single breath, he told me it was over. I was too ashamed to tell my parents and in the midst of my misery, OCD came flooding back suffusing me with intrusive thoughts.

I could not stop thinking about it. I felt that if I wasn't good enough for him then I was not good enough for anyone. I kept asking myself why this man had not given me his telephone number in Cardiff. I knew he owned two restaurants there and, shamefully, I also knew he was married, but surely he'd been telling me the truth when he told me his wife didn't understand him.

Some weeks later I got his telephone number from directory enquiries and somehow plucked up the courage to ring him. My heart pounded as I tapped my fingers in a safe sequence as the phone rang and rang. But he didn't answer the phone.

I could not let it go though and packed my bag leaving a letter for Mum and Dad and bought a train ticket to Cardiff. Once on the train my courage dissolved and I got off at the first stop which was Twyford. I called Mum from the phone booth and came home.

My parents sensibly didn't make much of this episode but it didn't stop my feelings of rejection, degradation and complete embarrassment of making such a fool of myself. What a silly little girl I'd been.

These feelings stayed with me until I decided to write a story called "Romance on the Riviera" and submit it to a teenage magazine that I read avidly each week. *Fab 208* is no longer published but at the time their editor loved my story and bought it from me, with copyright, for £50.

I felt as though my whole life was vindicated and that finally I was someone special. I kept telling myself that someone finally liked me, liked me enough to pay me to publish my story.

Unfortunately though that wasn't to be. The magazine folded before my "Romance on the Riviera" was published and in the process I lost the copyright. However, the Editor promised that if I came to see her when I was older, she would help me to get into the union and into magazine life.

I imagine that she never expected to see me again and so it wasn't surprising that she looked stunned when eighteen months later I took her at her word and made an appointment to see her at her office at IPC Magazines.

It took no more than ten minutes to ruin a year and a half's anticipation. Ten minutes to fob me off with reasons why she couldn't sponsor me for the union and in her haste to get rid of me, she finally called in one of her team and asked them to sponsor me.

The dignity I had carried with me into the office fell away as once again I felt an inadequate who had got in the way.

Two years on I was still feeling useless when I became embroiled in another unsuitable relationship which lasted a tempestuous two years with a man I'll call John.

He studied business at Newcastle Polytechnic (which is now called Metropolitan) and over the time we spent together, I must have travelled to see him almost thirty times. And how many times did he make the effort to be with me? None.

In my intense need to please, not only did I incur travel costs but also I took him food parcels. Even when he started pushing me about the warning bells didn't ring, as I was so grateful he loved me.

John's father was charming and polite but his stepmother was dominant and played cruel mind games with me. His father warned her to behave and John shouted at her, scaring me with his anger.

Nevertheless John and I spent an idyllic ten days in Cornwall, an oasis from the bleak bullying and arguing.

Eventually, with the help of a friend, I finished with him and with two of my girlfriends in tow, I went round to his parents' home to retrieve the expensive portable colour television I had bought John for poly. That evening he turned up drunk at my home carrying an empty bottle of vodka.

He wept as he sat on the stairs telling Dad how sorry he was for all the lies and the bullying and how he needed me. Dad tactfully pointed out that we'd had a difficult relationship and he'd not endeared himself to my parents, especially when he'd failed to pick me up at Hatch End Station at midnight.

I gently told John that it was finally over and there could be no resurrection.

Gradually I started going out again with friends and after a few months my cousin, Susan, told me that her boyfriend had a good friend called Brian. Susan arranged for us in a foursome to go for a meal in Harrow followed by a drink at The Travellers Rest in Kenton.

That same day, John rang and asked me to meet him which I did at the same restaurant I later went to in the foursome. The waiters certainly gave me knowing looks the second time I arrived as they must have thought I was quite a girl!

But not everything is as it seems and John actually did me a favour by meeting me that one last time as it reinforced my feelings to relegate him to my past and all I could think about was getting home to get ready for my date with Brian.

Brian and I hit it off immediately. There was no bolt from the blue, no one moment of falling in love, but within three weeks we were in love and two years later we married, on the 3rd March 1985.

Both of our mums said that when we first met we had both said about each other "he/she makes me laugh" and it's proved a good recipe for success. We've now been married for over twenty years and he's as much a part of me as is my right hand.

In those years I've doubted myself countless times, but I've never ever doubted Brian.

# Chapter 5
# MARRIED TO OCD

*It is not because things are difficult*
*that we do not dare, it is because we do not dare*
*that they are difficult*
*Seneca*

At the age of 23 I married my fiancé Brian, and we moved to our new home in Gants Hill, Ilford. I was now officially an Essex Girl. I was also no longer Alison Malnick; my new name was Alison Islin. I felt a sense of relief that at last I could hide from who I had been, as if this name-change had given me a new identity.

With married life came married responsibilities, and we fell swiftly into a convenient routine. Brian was working as a salesman for a big confectionery company, and I was working on *The Times* newspaper.

The position I held there was a union one. In those days the union in question was SOGAT, originally NATSOPA. My job was secretary to the two managing editors, Pat B Davis and Cyril Bainbridge. My responsibilities included looking after all of the foreign correspondents. Our department dealt with any problems they encountered whilst abroad. These could be financial, health, accommodation or even schools for their offspring.

We were rather like an adult's Mary Poppins for you name it and we provided it. We were called the Editorial Management Unit, but affectionately referred to as EMU.

I formed a friendship with the well known, and much acclaimed, Robert Fisk, the then Middle East correspondent based in The Lebanon in the capital Beirut. Often, when he was over, I would avidly listen to his wild tales of life in the front line and try to argue, reasonably, about how biased he was against Israel. It was always gentle and friendly and we never got heated.

I even invited Robert Fisk to my wedding to Brian. Unfortunately he could not make it, but it didn't stop him arriving at the office with our wedding present. He had brought us the most beautiful cutlery we had ever clapped eyes on, all the way from the Lebanon. I listened, transfixed, as he told me how it lay in the back of his four-wheel jeep as he was being pursued by would-be kidnappers!

I also came into constant contact, on an everyday basis, with the rest of the correspondents as our office ran their expenses and Pat or Cyril had to sign them before they could be authorised. Far from being rushed off my feet, I worked with a slightly more senior lady whereas the position only ever really required her job.

This is where my rituals entered into my working life. Perhaps if I had been busier then I wouldn't have had the time to perform them on a daily basis. Maybe if I had, then I would not have suffered as badly as I did.

I constantly punished myself with rituals that

seemed to sap all of my strength, mentally, physically, and, most of all, emotionally while I was typing up work for **Pat** or **Cyril**.

I would repeatedly type, tear-up, and retype the same letter or document, again and again and yet again. This would go on endlessly until I felt that I had performed the task to my complete satisfaction. I made sure that I screwed up each scribbled piece of paper into a tight ball so that the waste-paper basket didn't look too full. This made my workload seem heavier than it was. Although I knew it made me look extremely slow at my job to my bosses, I never stopped or even eased up as I performed each ritual, in my constant quest for perfection.

Whilst I was an employee of *The Times*, we were based in the Grays Inn Road, in London. There were many different corridors around our building leading to the various departments, be it the Home desk, Foreign desk, the Leader Writers office, the Letters Page etc. I always visited whichever location I had to by following the direction that my OCD would lead me, even if it was the long way round and I had to deliver something quickly.

My lunchtimes saw me ordering the same sandwich time and again, or if I was strolling across the river towards Fleet Street to meet a friend, checking the paving stones as I walked.

Surprisingly though, my OCD wasn't affected when a coded message from the IRA came through to the Foreign desk. Amid the general pandemonium I remained relatively calm – again it only confirms that logic has no bearing on OCD.

Looking back, the pressures of working, being married, having a new home, and indeed living in a new location, all contributed to the burden of my inner turmoil. I now cleaned my own home and found this took me about three quarters of a day.

To give you an idea of how I cleaned my cupboards I had to spray the inside roof of the cupboard, then the back panel, the left and then the right. Each one was sprayed three times, not in exactly the same place so I could see the separate drops trickling down. I then wiped each edge of the individual panels three times, culminating in wiping the centres of the panels three times vertically, three times horizontally and finally three times vertically.

It was inevitable that I inhaled some of the disinfectant spray and I developed a slight wheeze.

If the telephone or the doorbell interrupted me, I lost track of where I was and began again.

My self-esteem disappeared and with it any shred of self-worth that I might still have had.

Now was the time that the most disdainful ritual reared its ugly head and stayed with me for a long time. What was this ritual? Indeed, you may be shocked and disgusted as you read on. I positively forced myself to lick the bowl of the toilet wherever I was. This included loos at public places as well as at the homes of family and friends, and also at work.

I was convinced that if I did not do this ritual, then my brother would not be safe as he continued in his studies to become one of Israel's leading gastroenterologists. He was already a doctor, having done his degree at Oriel College, Oxford University, followed by his three years clinical at The Middlesex Hospital. I never told him any of this as I was too ashamed, but I fully believed his protection was in my control and the only way he'd stay safe was if I licked the toilet bowl.

Going out to my husband's family's functions

were traumatic for me as I felt ridiculed and my mother-in-law mocked my strange ways, sometimes tormenting me with her callous remarks for days on end.

I felt a failure. I had failed at school, letting the bullies beat me, and now I was being demeaned in a much more subtle way. I think that people began to see me as the girl sulking in the corner of the function, cutting herself off from everyone else. But the plain truth was that I felt frozen to the spot. I neither knew how to socialise nor how to laugh any more.

So, going home I would indulge myself with more rituals because they helped me to keep some kind of control on the situation. I knew deep down that no one had really ever had the chance to get to know the real Alison; not as a Malnick, nor now as an Islin.

As time went on I became convinced that if we had a baby then I would miraculously become a different person. Yes, this would be the making of me. At long last there would be a genuine reason to get up in the morning. Someone would depend on me for his or her very existence. As in the days of my Julie doll, I would be needed.

We started trying for a baby after only four months of marriage. I was sure that I would be unable to conceive as a punishment for being me. As it happens I did have some treatment but after eight months of trying I conceived naturally.

Now the dangerous games really began. I would pull the muscles in my stomach upwards and out, if that makes any sense. I don't know the reason I invented this one, but I ended up with constant aches in the muscular area of my stomach.

Some time into my pregnancy, after I had managed to stop punishing my unborn child for my heavy guilt trip, I started to relax a little and I even began to enjoy my rapidly expanding baby-bump.

One friend gave birth to a son and developed post-natal depression amongst other things. I decided to write to her while she was in hospital. The simple task of writing a comforting and amusing letter took sixteen attempts. I was hot, uncomfortable and sure that I was causing stress to my own unborn baby as this particular ritual took up most of one whole day.

Finally, our baby's birth day arrived and we called our beautiful, healthy son Mark Robert.

Although I'd been racked with fear as to how my OCD would take over once the baby was born, surprisingly it seemed to be in recession and I was able to keep it under control for a few weeks.

I was happy. But I couldn't accept it and felt that somehow I'd be punished for being like this. Bad enough that I'd been degraded enough to lick the toilet, I now did something a million times worse.

I convinced myself that my punishment would be that I'd lose my baby. So somehow I started to rationalise it and reasoned with myself all the ways I could possibly lose my son. Of course illness and terrible accidents wouldn't be down to me so I felt the only course left would be that I would harm my precious little boy. The more I thought about it, the more real it became and I convinced myself that I eventually would end up killing my baby.

I couldn't enjoy my time with my baby; after all what would-be murderer had the right to be happy? Then it happened when Mark was just a few weeks old. I can hardly bear to admit this for when he was asleep I took a sharp kitchen knife and lightly touched his sleeping head with it, just on top of his forehead, near his eyes.

I now had shame on top of all my other phobias and this stayed with me until several years later when Dr Veale told me that what I'd done was a classic example of behaviour therapy. Not only that, but he was very pleased with me. Those wasted years of beating myself up were all for nothing.

I was getting more and more withdrawn and introverted. I didn't want to make friends, because I didn't deserve to have friends. After a few months, Brian became concerned about me and felt that the answer would be to move back to north west London where I had grown up. We settled on Edgware, a new place and yet another new start.

But how wrong we were; if life was bleak in Essex it was nothing compared with how I was after the move. I felt desperate but couldn't explain why, not even to myself. All I know is that I stopped actively living my life and began merely to exist.

On the occasional day when I actually made the effort to put on make-up I'd not bother to take it off before I went to bed. I rarely showered or washed my hair. I spent most of my time ritualising – not because I wanted to but because I had no choice.

I even had to use toilet paper in a certain order. Rather like a child obeying the Green Cross Code, I had to use three sheets in front, three at back and three at front again. Last thing at night I'd have to flush the toilet time and time again, sometimes having to ask Brian to check that I'd really flushed it. I even remember standing at the cistern with the handle broken off in my hand after repeated flushing.

I felt like I was flying freefall with no parachute and there was no way back.

# Chapter 6
# TENTATIVE STEPS TOWARDS RECOVERY

*We must accept finite disappointment,*
*but we must never lose infinite hope*
*Martin Luther King*

At this time my parents were best friends with a lovely couple who lived in Hackney. My mother and Pamela had met at school and remained close throughout the years. Pam's husband Bernard was a GP, and my mother sought advice from him as to whether I could be treated.

Bernard wanted to help and arranged for me to see a psychiatrist. Brian took me every week at 8 am and waited with the baby in the car. And this was where I first learned that I had OCD. It was such a relief to know that I wasn't mad, and furthermore that I wasn't alone. After all, if someone had bothered to put a name to it, then I couldn't be the only sufferer. I felt like shouting out loud that I could finally see that none of this was my fault.

I knew that if I had a broken arm at least it would have made sense, not only to other people but to me too. A plaster cast or a sling would have been a sign that, although fractured, the bone was healing.

And now it felt almost as though a balm was being soothed into my mind, reassuring me that I wasn't alone any more. That other people also knew how it felt if a tin of beans stood upside down or if the bathroom towels didn't hang with their labels uniformly showing. Although I didn't think I had some imaginary power or that some great ill would happen if the beans weren't the right way up or the towels were skew-whiff in the bathroom, it made me feel uncomfortable to such a degree that I'd brood or ruminate on it for the rest of the day.

Like a victim giving into a blackmailer, it was so much easier to succumb to the urge to rearrange the towels or turn the can of beans the other way up than to have the picture of them dancing in my head until I tried, unsuccessfully, to sleep later that night.

I now knew that I wasn't alone; that others understood that I had to clear my mind in order to be free to take on the next disturbance.

However, my euphoria was short-lived. Instead of dealing with the OCD, the doctor considered that Brian and I needed sexual therapy and by an amazing coincidence, he also practised as a Sex Therapist!

Brian was prepared to give anything a try by this stage, and we tried it once but never again. We were asked intimate questions about our love life such as "How often do you make love?" "What foreplay do you enjoy?" "Do you have oral sex?"

We were then given various exercises to work on between that and our next session, such as how we should stroke each other. But we couldn't see the connection between rituals and sex and never bothered to go back.

Once diagnosed with OCD I coped reasonably

well and even managed to have a part-time job a couple of mornings and afternoons each week working in a children's clothes shop in Temple Fortune while my mother babysat Mark.

Like any other shop assistant, I was careful to ensure that all the buttons and zips were as they should be. But other salesladies wouldn't have been flustered if two hangers touched each other or a button wasn't pushed all the way through or the top of the zip wasn't lying flat.

Again, as in the days when I was at The Times, my OCD affected my work. However it didn't immobilise me and I managed to carry on.

Brian and I even felt it was the right time for another baby and I was fortunate enough to conceive again.

I faced up to a new beginning with more enthusiasm than I'd been able to muster for years. My only problem was Mark, who was a very difficult toddler; at times I found myself smacking him too hard.

But my days of happiness were not to last very long as about six weeks into pregnancy I miscarried. I felt that my baby was a scapegoat, and that I was the real target. The pain I felt was indescribable; somehow I was not surprised to feel it physically as well as emotionally. However, the pain in my stomach became more severe and just before I rang the hospital they contacted me to say that from the examination of my miscarriage, I had had an ectopic pregnancy and I needed to be admitted immediately.

My surgeon was the new-age gynaecologist, Yehudi Gordon, who successfully removed my right fallopian tube. But he didn't realize when he told me that it was possible that if I conceived again there would be a high risk of a further ectopic pregnancy how he triggered my OCD.

All I could think was that I'd lose my other fallopian tube and never be able to have another child. The "what if's" began to scream out at me; what if Mark was run over and died, what if Mark had a terrible illness and died, what if Mark were murdered ... these thoughts were played over and over in my head and I found I couldn't get through the simplest of tasks. I cried constantly because I couldn't see any future as Mr Gordon couldn't guarantee that my beloved son wouldn't be murdered or meet with a fatal illness or accident.

Becoming concerned, he called a Harley Street psychiatrist to see me. He put me on an anti-psychotic drug called Haloperidol and fixed a date for me to see him on my discharge from The Garden Hospital.

More dazed than functioning, I put my life on hold while I waited for this new wonder drug to take effect. And boy! It certainly had an effect. My tongue started to take on a life of its own. Almost immediately my top lip completely straightened, getting rid of the heart shape you have in the middle. My tongue fell out of my mouth, and completely hung down against my bottom lip.

I was so distressed that Brian tried to contact the specialist but it was Christmas Eve and we couldn't get hold of him. We were told to go to our local hospital's A&E. We shot off to Edgware General and I sat very close to Brian, unhappily aware of the other patients staring at me as I must have looked demented.

Finally, after what seemed like hours, the doctor saw me and said I needed an antidote to counteract the reaction I had had from the drug. As we drove home my tongue gradually returned to my mouth, and my lip started to go back to its normal shape too.

To my relief the only after effects I suffered were aches at the back of my tongue, the result of the length of time it had been dangling from my mouth.

I was still in touch with Mr Gordon and I'll always be grateful to him. He had fixed more than my body; I went home after the operation with lots of coping strategies and contacts who would help me. I began to have fertility treatment with Mr Gordon and his partner Faith Haddad at the Garden Hospital.

It truly was a time of healing as I started seeing a private psychotherapist every week to sort out my life. We talked about the bullying I'd suffered as a child and even tried to get a grip on my rituals. We talked about my whole life, even down to my failed relationship with my mother-in-law and extended family.

Thanks to the fertility drug Clomid, about six months later I discovered I was pregnant again. I sailed through my pregnancy to such an extent I even stopped smacking Mark.

Perhaps because I was on such a high, I wanted everything about this pregnancy to be perfect. I even opted for a water birth. And now, with Mitchell Craig our family was complete.

# Chapter 7
# ONE STEP FORWARD, TWO STEPS BACK

*Our greatest glory is not in never failing,*
*but in rising up every time we fail*
*Ralph Waldo Emerson*

It all sounds pretty much like fairyland, doesn't it. The once obsessive mother who was now in complete control with her perfect family. Unfortunately nothing was as it seemed.

The crunch came when I had to face that I was failing both as a wife and mother to my two little boys. Mark was 5 and Mitchell was 2 and they had a mother who couldn't cope.

My daily compulsions began before I even got up in the morning. My bedside clock was a digital football with a pink face and if it showed the time as being anything ending with a 7 or had digits combining 7 (such as 43 or 52) then I couldn't get up until the minute had passed. Thankfully, it was only the minutes that mattered and not the hour, so I could get up between 6.59 and 8.00. Well, I could so long as it wasn't 7.25 or 7.27.

I had to get both in and out of the shower with my right foot first I had to examine the soap for any hairs stuck on it, both before and after I'd used it, and scrupulously remove any I found.

I washed my hair and body as regimentally as any sergeant major would wish to see his platoon marching.

Once I had got out of the shower - right foot first - I had to meticulously dry myself. No flat pack furniture comes with such complicated instructions as those I would have to prepare if I were to explain precisely how I dried myself. Back, arms, neck, breasts, nipples, and belly – I rubbed until I was chafed and red. No part of my body would escape the onslaught from my towel.

All the money invested in M&S marketing for lingerie, the prettiest colours, pinks, blues, lilacs, the embroidered floral designs etc, was wasted on me. I could only wear white underwear. My knickers and bras were so stark on my washing line that neighbours must have thought I was signalling my surrender.

To dress, I laid my knickers and bra on Brian's side of the bed, first examining them for the tiniest hair or particle of fluff. If I caught my big toe into my knickers as I was putting them on, you'd have thought I was dancing the okey cokey as I had to put my leg in and out three times.

I should have had a stomach that even Cher or Jane Fonda would have envied because when I made the bed my self-imposed discipline was to hold my stomach in to the count of 50. I ignored the phone or even the children crying out for me – nothing was allowed to interrupt my half-century of counting.

As you know, children love aping their parents, especially their mothers. They take on their parents' mannerisms when they speak into their toy telephones or put their hands on their hips when they get frustrated and reprimand their toys as we have reprimanded them; all part of innocent childhood.

But nothing prepared me for seeing Mitchell tapping his little foot three times or walking backwards and forwards in time with me, as I performed my rituals. He began to develop his own rituals and, like a mother who knows her nicotine habit is suffusing her child with smoke but cannot quit the habit, nothing could stop me from this all-consuming force. No nothing, not even my love for my child could stop it.

The upshot was that the fatigue from merely getting showered and dressed and then spending two hours wiping down the kitchen units made me not want to cook or even look after my boys. My rituals dominated every hour of not only my day but to my horror I even found myself performing rituals in my dreams.

Again I lost all self-respect and neglected my appearance. I was unkempt, barely bothering to wash or wear make-up. Worst of all, I felt myself becoming remote from my boys.

Little by little all self-control ebbed away. I began losing my temper with Mark, not because I was annoyed with him but I was angry with myself. I knew I wasn't a child batterer, how could I be? But if I wasn't, then why was I smacking my child? The defining moment came when Mark bounced on my bed and I smacked him so vigorously that he fell to the floor. That was it, I knew I needed help.

I forced myself to see my GP, Dr Krasner. He has since been a constant source of help and support. He referred me for an assessment to Dr Veale at Edgware General Hospital. This was the first time I'd heard of Dr Veale, the man who has become such a cornerstone of my life.

Dr Veale could see that I needed to be treated as an inpatient for about a month and as I am fortunate enough to be insured with BUPA I agreed to go into The Priory rather than be added to the NHS waiting list.

However, it was not quite as straightforward as it sounds because my compulsions intervened and I reluctantly told Dr Veale I could only come into hospital after 31$^{st}$ December 1992 as we were still in a leap year. I could not begin to explain why, but leap years still remain a stumbling block to me. But we were already in December so I persuaded the Doctor to admit me into The Priory in January.

Now I had another problem; although I'd not been the perfect mother at least I'd been around and now I had to make arrangements for them to be looked after in my absence. My only thought was for my parents to take over as best they could. The first stumbling block was that my Dad, a keen walker and rambler, didn't own a car. So Brian insured my Nissan Sunny for Dad.

Dad would drop Mum off at our home first thing on Monday to Friday mornings and collect her again early evening. This enabled Brian to go to work as normal and saved the children's routine, such as it was at that stage, from being interrupted. Mum fed them breakfast, took Mark to infant school and Mitchell to nursery. Although Mum cooked and kept the house tidy, she didn't need to do any cleaning as by then, to meet the demands of my ever-increasing rituals we had struggled to find the money to take on a cleaning lady.

After school, Mum would set about entertaining the boys and their friends to keep them from missing me and fretting.

All this meant that I was free to concentrate purely on getting better. Most of my life though I'd lived within a prison of OCD – was it possible that now the cell doors would be unlocked and I would be released?

# Chapter 8
## FACING MY DEMONS

*My psychiatrist told me I've got OCD.*
*I told him I wanted a second opinion.*
*He told me, "OK, you're ugly too"*
*Anon*

That's how I came to be huddled in the back of Brian's car as he drove me up Dracula's Drive that freezing morning in January 1993.

I settled well into The Priory, forcing myself to relax into the surrounding opulence and to allow myself to enjoy the "me" time. That was the greatest luxury of all; not the ornate domed ceilings or gold leaf paint but it was time out, time out for me.

After that first lunch when Bob had insisted that he wasn't a frog, I fled to my room and listened to a tape that Dr Veale had previously recorded.

His soft, comforting voice was healing and he spoke so much sense that I found myself hungry for more and more knowledge about my jailer, OCD. And as I listened I began to learn. I knew this was my chance to get well, and I was going to do all I could to succeed.

*The Priory*

There was one slight hiccup which was probably avoidable but I hated letting people down, even if it hurt me in the process. We had booked a weekend to Centre Parks with a family we'd met a few months previously in Cyprus. We didn't know them well, and I felt guilty about letting them down.

As I was allowed to leave The Priory for the weekend there seemed no reason to cancel. Brian did all the packing and collected me on the Friday morning. I was equipped with pens and paper for my homework and I tried to convince myself all would be well, but the truth was that I was scared. After just four days in hospital I no longer felt safe outside the sanctuary of Room 13.

We met up with our friends and had lunch together. I felt myself relaxing and while in the pool that afternoon I confided to my friend that I was actually a psychiatric patient and was enjoying a weekend break. She was horrified, and from then on she tried to keep clear of me.

I began to see myself through her eyes, and by Sunday I felt such a freak that I could hardly speak and begged Brian to take me back to our room.

I was not due back at The Priory until the Monday morning, but I felt such revulsion at the thought that anyone else would see me that I pleaded with Brian to take me back early.

Brian dropped me off outside The Priory. He dropped me outside because I told him I didn't want him to come in with me. It never occurred to me how my constant rejection hurt him as I was unable to move outside my own fears and humiliations.

Peggy, another patient, saw me looking dejected and asked me into her room. She and her husband John only needed to take one look at me to realize the break had come much too soon. I couldn't face them and I shook my head sadly and took my bag back to my room. I refused to speak to the nurses. All I wanted was to be left alone.

I remember a time during the first four weeks of my stay at The Priory when I felt particularly vulnerable and ran distressed into Peggy's arms. I didn't speak to her. I just clung on to her and placed my wedding and engagement rings into her hand, closing her fingers around them protectively. I didn't think myself worthy of continuing to wear them. At least I hope that is all I was thinking.

During my stay at the hospital I had intensive cognitive behaviour therapy (CBT) every day with various consultants, including Professor Windy Dryden.

We were a big group, varying from fourteen to

twenty people. We met for three hours, during which each of us stated a major worry.

For instance, if I said I was worried nobody liked me, Professor Dryden would ask me how it made me feel. I would then learn how to challenge these negative beliefs.

Although my worries have changed over fourteen years, I still use the technique that helps turn a negative way of thinking into a more positive one.

One task Professor Dryden gave me was to write a hierarchy list. This was a full and comprehensive list of all my obsessions, compulsions and fears relating to my performing of rituals. I had to write it as the thoughts came to me and then rewrite it in an order that reflected my levels of anxiety. The idea was that we would start tackling the easier obstacles before, eventually, being able to face the toughest of the toughest.

Having chosen a particular number to deal with, I then had to put the theory into practice. For example, I might choose "fear of touching the outside dustbin and then not being allowed to wash my hands". I would then have to come into the house and touch various objects at random. I wouldn't be able to wash my hands for the next 45 minutes.

I had to record the level of anxiety this would cause me on a scale of 1 to 100. The level would start high but as the next three quarters of an hour passed I was able to notice the excessively high levels decrease to a much more acceptable and manageable pace.

It was during these sessions that I began to learn about myself and even began to like myself, something I'd not have thought possible.

## ASSIGNMENT TASK

Name: A. Islo    Date: 14/2/1993   Negotiated with: MZ

**AGREED TASK** - State the task and when, where and how frequently you have agreed to do it:

Clear Wardrobe — Sort out clothes, hang-ups and folded.

## THE THERAPEUTIC PURPOSE(S) OF THE TASK:

To feel a sense of orderliness and to help with laziness. Make things tidier and neater.

## OBSTACLES TO CARRYING OUT THE TASK - What obstacles, if any, stand in your way of completing this task and how you can overcome them:

1. Finding time — I'll do it somehow.
2. Energy — Tackle it and See.
3. Motivation — Do it early whilst awake!
4. The Patience — Just persevere.
5. Waiting to begin — Just do it.

## WHAT I ACTUALLY DID AND LEARNED:

I did it. But I was plagued with folding rituals and tapping hangers. Banged right leg with clothing. I could have achieved this task in 45 minutes, whereas it took 2 hours I feel disappointed in myself.    Signed: A. Ast

# *Working through my OCD*

Occupational therapy, much to my great surprise, was extremely rewarding. I'm known in my family as a lousy artist but I managed to produce two very acceptable brooches as souvenirs for my children.

By this time Dr Veale decided that as I'd worked through some of the easier rituals, it was time to help me combat my concerns about harming my children.

Rationally I knew I never would hurt my children but that part of me that was governed by OCD couldn't be sure. Like an actress who ignores the dozens of complimentary critiques about her performance, yet only believes the one containing a slur, no amount of reassurance could make me rationalise the situation realistically.

During an occupational therapy class I painted a vivid picture of myself harming my little boy. I was made to stick this on the wall in my room. Instead of provoking another attack of ritualising, I discovered that confronting fear is the only way to face up to things. Even better, because of my appalling artwork, I found myself laughing at the picture.

Mind you, I soon stopped laughing when faced with my next task.

I hadn't heard of a loop tape before. It's a cassette that runs for several seconds and then keeps rewinding and starting again and again until you press the stop button.

I had to speak into the thirty-second tape graphically describing how I would murder my son.

I don't know what was the worst part; preparing beforehand all I would say and to fit it into 30 seconds or to sit in my room with headphones on and listen to my murder repeating itself continuously for 45 minutes.

The first few minutes of hearing the tape were probably the hardest thing I've ever done, but incredibly, rather like morning fog, the horror began to lift. By the end of the session I was actually drifting off into planning my younger son's birthday party.

And that's how this therapy worked. I began to relax while listening to the tape, and I finally came to acknowledge that a thought was just that - a thought, and not an action.

I had another seemingly pointless fear and that was of carrier bags. I was scared that in my sleep I would suffocate in one. So why was I surprised to discover the arrival of countless bags that were duly deposited around my room? And again it worked.

Although I faced some traumatic experiences, I had some lovely moments as well while at The Priory. Daily, before breakfast, we would meet up at reception and be invited to have a walk around the lake in Groveland's Park.

The house was pretty splendid, having been built in 1797 to the designs of John Nash. General Pinochet was held under house arrest while a patient there.

The grounds were landscaped by Humphrey Renton and are quite sensational. The park comprises a wooded area, with a pumped stream that flows from a lake, a grassed area including several football pitches, a children's playground, a pavilion and a small aviary.

The scenery was breathtaking in January and early February and we all felt uplifted seeing the ducks and the different birds gliding along the lake. The air was fresh and although it was quite chilly, we were warmed by the briskness of our jaunt.

I joined the keep-fit class for some gentle

exercise and attended classes on assertiveness, living skills, stress and anxiety. By now I was referring to The Priory as my Mental Health Farm.

I was given set assignments to complete. For example, one was for Brian to bring the boys to see me and for me to bath them.

When I was home I had simple tasks to plan, such as taking the boys to the local park or reading with them and sorting out our dirty laundry.

You may think that they sound too simple to even be called a task but during any sort of mental distress, any task you would normally do on automatic pilot makes you feel that you're actually flying the plane.

I could barely keep awake or focus on anything, which was probably due to the anti-depressant I was on. Did it stop me feeling depressed? It probably stopped me feeling anything at all except for panic that I couldn't look after my two young children.

Although I went on Seroxat (Paroxetine) when I was first admitted into The Priory, it hadn't agreed with me and I switched to Clomipramine (Anafranil) which is from the Tricyclic drug family.

Dr Veale decided to readmit me for two weeks and I was given the same drug but intravenously through a vein in my arm daily for about an hour a time. This way the drug bypassed my liver and was absorbed into my bloodstream more quickly. It seemed to do the trick because after the fortnight I was finally discharged properly.

I think the more modern preference for treatment for OCD is to treat it with much newer drugs called Selective Serotonin Reuptake Inhibitors (SSRI's). They seem to have fewer side-effects than mine but it was important for me to go onto a medication that was well-tested.

I gradually worked on my self-concept, which is how I viewed myself and how I felt others saw me. I kept a regular inventory on my depression using various charts to monitor my continuing progress. I learnt to recognise when I was on the "downward spiral" and had an arsenal of techniques to help me cope.

I discovered that I couldn't talk myself through the depression but I had to write it all down. Somehow, seeing it made the difference; it made it real. I'm sure that many of you have gone shopping and forgotten your list, but the process of having written everything down made it easier to recall.

Gradually I learnt to do the cognitive behaviour therapy by myself without a therapist which was the turning point. I used CBT when I felt no one liked me or that I was a bad person. Other times were when I felt useless and no good to anyone or that I wasn't capable of doing anything.

Not only did CBT control the negative emotions but it also led me to a more positive way of thinking and has now become a way of life. Rather like people who are completely bi-lingual and aren't always aware which language they're speaking, I now reach out for CBT without even realizing it.

If I am honest though it doesn't work in every part of my day. For instance when I go shopping I have to place my purchases on the conveyor belt in order. Toiletries, cleaning products, fresh food, fruit with fruit, vegetables all together, frozen food next to each other and so on.

It probably sounds logical as it is easier to unpack and is something most people do. The main difference with me is that I have to do it religiously including placing everything the correct way up on the conveyor belt and also in the shopping bags.

An example of improvement rather than complete cure is that I now no longer write off five days each month when I menstruate.

My periods still affect me though to a lesser extent. In the past I couldn't read during them as I have obsessive thoughts of blood and contamination and I'd forever associate such a book with blood. Now, although I can't start a new book, at least I'm able to continue reading one I've already started.

On the fifth day of my period I have to strip the whole bed, even the mattress and protector, and wash it all on a 90 degree wash, no matter whether or not it needs to be done. I also have to wash all the trousers I've worn over my period.

Less logically, when the dustmen call on Thursday I need them to empty the bin completely. If they leave anything in it, even a piece of paper, I have to lay the bin on its side and crawl in to retrieve whatever's left. I am compelled to get in my car and throw the offending item in a street bin outside my immediate neighbourhood.

At one point if I so much as saw someone wiping their nose and there was blood on the tissue it would spoil my day and if I were well into a book I'd have to leave it and not read it again.

Actually, reading a book was a minefield for me. Even though I was reading it to myself, I'd have to put stress on the correct syllables and I could reread the same page up to a dozen times till I got it right.

To stop myself checking and reading a particular passage over and over, I frequently ended up tearing out the page but I'd then feel compelled to get it back and had to buy another copy of the book.

To try to help with my obsessions about blood, Dr Veale took some blood from my arm and I had to carry it around in a little phial. What he didn't know until now is that I threw it into a dustbin as soon as I could!

Rather like the actress who said it took twenty years to become an overnight success, my path to recovery has been fraught with pitfalls and hurdles but now I focus on the future and don't waste precious moments mulling over what has gone.

# Chapter 9
## BREAKING FREE

*Hope is like a bird that senses the dawn*
*and carefully starts to sing while it is still dark*
*Anon*

Recovery is an ongoing process. Although I was discharged from The Priory some fourteen years ago, like a recovering alcoholic I still take life one day at a time. I think I always will.

If I feel low which could lead to a downward spiral into depression, I take a form of avoidance action which I am trying to curb. I rush to the shops and buy three large bars of chocolate which, if anyone comments, I pretend are for my children.

I hurry back to the car whilst my heart is racing and I'm getting hotter and hotter, and I tear the wrappers and shovel it in without even tasting it. I'm so desperate that I can't even wait till I get home.

Naturally the guilt then sets in and I hate myself for giving in to this addiction. The only difference between my eating disorder and a bulimic is that I don't vomit it up afterwards.

It is happening less though and like a latter day Pollyanna, I am a believer in turning bad into good; rather than deny OCD, I've turned it into a career, a way of life. For a year after I left hospital I saw Rob Wilson, a brilliant clinical psychologist who turned out to be as dedicated and gifted at helping me as Doctor Veale. They've turned me from a victim into a woman with a future.

When I left The Priory Dr Veale asked me to set up a Support Group within the confines of the hospital grounds. Now some fourteen years later I believe it is the longest running OCD support group in the UK. I am still running it and it continues to grow in popularity. Between six and twenty six members attend each month with an average of around sixteen people. We are affiliated to the charity OCD Action and the group is listed with various other governing bodies.

Occasionally we have a guest speaker, for whom we always have a good response. When the TV film *Dirty Filthy Love* was being made, three of the actors came to our two-hour meeting to get an insight into how OCD affects sufferers.

After seven years of running the group I found I was craving to be more involved in the world of general mental health. I joined Barnet Voice, a user-run and user-staffed organisation; to be involved you have to have, or have had, some form of mental distress. Our reason for existence is to try to improve mental health services within Barnet. I believe there are similar groups all over the world.

I now go on the wards of Edgware and Barnet Psychiatric Hospitals doing outreach. Outreach is all about going on the wards with in-patients to find out how they are coping and how they are finding their care and treatment. Within the limits of what we can do, we help them with any problems they feel are not being met.

I run a weekly support group with a wonderful man called Robert. This is for anyone suffering mental distress in the community. I have also recently become involved in junior doctor training and am hoping to be involved in interviewing for hospital posts. I now find that I have become conscious of how many people are affected in some way, with one in four people suffering some form of mental problem.

Barnet Voice have also invested in the purchase of a house to be set up as a weekend respite facility for people in the community who suffer a crisis in their mental health. We will be the first organisation to provide this sort of support in the Borough of Barnet.

What I have found is no different from what mental health patients the world over have discovered. If I had suffered with an illness such as cancer or had an accident or operation, then compassion would flow like a fountain. But if I tell people I have a mental health problem then, even now, people mentally take a step back.

When I was first officially diagnosed with OCD I felt a surge of elation along with the fear. Elation because if my condition had a name then I couldn't be the only one suffering from it and fear because if I had a mental condition then that had to make me mental.

I can honestly say, though, that having OCD has shaped my life and, for good or bad, it has made me the person I am today.

Oddly enough, OCD has had one unexpected upshot. I've always considered that I had an unhappy childhood, primarily because I have no positive memories of growing up. On the other hand, my brother has only good thoughts of those times

As a measure of how I have now begun to take control of my life, I realize that my childhood was, in fact, no different from Stephen's but the bullying and victimisation wrapped around my good memories like an insidious creeper suffocating a prize rose bush.

Had it not been for OCD I wouldn't be involved with The Priory or any of the other mental health work I do or people I have come to meet through it. But above all, I have learnt to respect every kind of illness, physical, mental and emotional. Each ailment is just that.

It is people's fear of the unknown and fear of being labelled that frightens them off and causes hostility and isolation to so many people. After all, no matter our symptoms we are all human beings and can still hear, see and feel the fear and negativity that exists in so many of us.

As I mentioned, one in four will suffer some kind of mental distress at some time in their lives. Think about it, one in four. There is a saying that you should think of three friends and if it isn't one of them, then it could well be you!

Between 2% and 3% of the global population suffer to some degree with OCD and as Dr Veale pointed out in his foreword, OCD is listed in the top ten most debilitating illnesses according to the World Health Organisation.

Sadly, no one is immune and being stigmatised for something that is not your fault adds to the feelings of isolation and guilt. Verbal abuse and condemnation merely feed an illness when what are needed are support and compassion and understanding.

Please remember this should someone in your own family or circle of friends become ill.

I have now reached a stage in my life that I thought would never come. I finally feel comfortable in my own skin. I've learnt to stop apologising for being me, and for the first time I actually rather like myself.

Indeed I would go further than that, I respect the woman I have become.

Brian continues to provide me with the support and love that makes our marriage the focal point of my life. My two boys have grown into fine young men that any mother would be proud to call "son".

As well as working in mental health, I also have the confidence to work part-time in a top department store and, as when I worked in Temple Fortune all those years ago, I again work with clothes.

I'm what is known as a floater which means I go to various departments when they are short staffed, possibly due to sickness or holidays. Because of this I don't always work on the fashion floor but occasionally work on my two favourite departments, Gifts and Toiletries. Here I feel more relaxed and possibly less threatened.

I call the fashion floor *the city* because it's hectic and I am still faced with the same rituals that I performed in Temple Fortune, although not on the same scale. I call the other two floors *the countryside* as they make me feel more relaxed, especially on the lower ground floor where I can smell the scents of the various candles and perfumes.

When I am cashing up at the end of my shift, I tend to count some of the coins up to three times to make sure I have made no errors. All the notes have to be round the same way and I am like that, too, when serving customers. I can't open the till to give change or close it without making certain that all notes are positioned correctly and no stray coins have escaped to the wrong sections.

So yes, there are certain rituals that I still perform although nowadays I prefer to call them 'routines'. As I have said before, OCD rears its head during times of stress, and although I am now about 80% recovered, I do still have the odd period that is bleak, pretty much like anyone with an addictive personality.

I think that the main way ritualising has affected me is that I do it in order to get rid of negative thoughts, which are often to do with any kind of rejection from work to family and friends.

I know I internalise situations and blame myself for whatever goes wrong, agonising over them. This sort of negativity is common amongst people who suffer with any kind of mental distress.

It makes me ritualise harder and faster than I would normally so I get some semblance of keeping control.

I'm nowhere near as self-deprecating as I once was though. I've learnt through psychotherapy and CBT that I'm not the one who's always responsible for failed relationships although I do still tend to be more defensive than I probably should be. I know it's a form of protection but gradually I'm laying down my shields.

I believe I have found the right balance in my career path. Mind you, nothing matches working in mental health for me and I know it is a privilege to be allowed into people's lives during what is often a distressing time for them.

Surely the icing on my cake is my two most beautiful West Highland terriers Gracie and Freddie whom we all adore. Each day, as I walk them round the park I look around at the changing seasons and simply enjoy breathing in the fresh air. My boys laugh at me when I tell them to look at the trees and it takes me back to when I laughed at my Dad who used to say the same things to me.

But I feel that every second of my life must be valued because I have lost so much of it to OCD and I know how precious every moment is.

I go swimming and to yoga classes. I have learnt that keeping my body healthy keeps my mind focussed on what is important. Even a short time spent walking, swimming or on yoga is so rewarding and you don't need to join a gym or run a marathon for exercise to be beneficial.

I swim forty lengths each week in an Olympic size pool at my local leisure centre. It normally takes me about fifty minutes and my reward is the adrenalin buzz I get afterwards.

However, I am not able to leave my OCD in the locker along with my jeans and trainers. Although friends have suggested they come with me, I refuse their company, as I need to count the lengths I swim and friends would talk and I would lose count.

Even so if I think I have lost count, I add rather than subtract a number so although I may have swam more than forty lengths, I won't have swam less.

If I were asked to sum up my description of living with OCD I would say:

Many years of my early life were spent locked away in a mental prison. Physically I was there but inside my head were steel bars and no matter how hard I tried to break free, those bars never budged.

I functioned in the same way I breathed but never actually lived. Nevertheless I survived and now I have a second chance.

I know that I am blessed at last. Yes, it took a long time coming but I have discovered that my happiness comes through my health and my family's health. Cliché? Probably, but clichés are simply oft repeated truths.

I think that what I would most share with you is that I no longer live in fear, dependent on non-existent guarantees and certainties. I now live for today and relish the good times, instead of looking over my shoulder forever dominated by obsessions.

I can truthfully say that OCD is no longer my jailer. If I had the choice, I wouldn't wish not to have had it as it's given me so much. I now have a career, an insight and the opportunity to help others.

Yes, OCD still affects me but no, it no longer has power over me.

Finally Alison Islin is in control.

*When I look into the future,*
*it's so bright it burns my eyes*

*Oprah Winfrey*

# OCD, MY FRIEND

I wasn't very old when it surfaced
masked by numerous disguises.
My journeys lengthened daily, whilst my mind,
encapsulated by rituals, worked overtime.

"Did I check it?" "Should I check it?"
"Do I really care?"
But no, OCD, my friend the parasite,
has grown over the years
breeding with my personality
thus becoming my soul mate.

Sometimes my day disabled beyond compare,
counting, washing,
playing dodgems with my footsteps
in the rash hope disaster won't occur
keeping normality from my door.
Debilitating and frighteningly menacing
OCD destroying any previous career.

But I have salvaged from the remnants of my past
a new strength,
an inner wisdom
to accept there are no certainties in life.
Medication, CBT, exposure therapy
and a tremendous amount of hard work
have gained me a future,
not entirely void of OCD,
but freeing my mind from standing still,
introducing the negatives to the positives, and now,
OCD my friend, you can live in my shadows,
and I can move on.

©1999 Alison Islin

# GLOSSARY

CLINICAL PSYCHOLOGIST - Licenced mental health professional (Ph.D. or Psy.D.) who specializes in the evaluation, diagnosis, and treatment of mental disorders. The term was introduced in a 1907 paper by the American psychologist Lightner Witmer (1867-1956).

COGNITIONS - Thoughts or beliefs.

COGNITIVE BEHAVIOUR THERAPY - Cognitive therapy or cognitive behaviour therapy is a kind of psychotherapy used to treat OCD, depression, anxiety disorders, phobias, and other forms of mental disorder. It involves recognising distorted thinking and learning to replace it with more realistic substitute ideas.

EXPOSURE THERAPY - Exposure therapy is a process in which the phobic person is exposed to the feared situations or objects. The therapy may be done "in vivo" (the person is actually exposed to the real situations or objects) or through visualisation techniques. Exposure therapy reduces the physical or emotional distress you experience when confronted with a particular object, situation, or distressing thought or memory.

LOOP-TAPE - Loops of pre-recorded magnetic tape used to create repetitive talking, singing or rhythmic musical patterns. A length of recorded magnetic tape is cut and spliced end to end, creating a circle or loop that can be played continuously, usually on a reel-to-reel machine. Loop tapes can also work with cassette recorders.

**OBSESSIVE COMPULSIVE DISORDER** - Obsessions are the thoughts. The compulsions are the performing of the rituals. Can have mental rituals as well as physical ones. Alison has them in her dreams.

**PSYCHIATRIST** - A medical doctor who specializes in the diagnosis and treatment of mental disorders.

**RITUALS** - With obsessive compulsive disorder (OCD), you develop disturbing, obsessive thoughts that cause fear or anxiety. In order to rid yourself of these thoughts and relieve the fear, you perform rituals, such as repeated hand washing or checking. Unfortunately, the relief is only temporary. The thoughts return and you repeat the rituals. The rituals or behaviours become time-consuming and have a significant impact on your daily life.

**RUMINATIONS OR INTRUSIVE THOUGHTS** - Many people have occasional, strange thoughts about violent or unhappy things. They are only odd thoughts that flit through our brains. People don't usually talk about these thoughts, but they are very common and don't mean much of anything. They don't hurt anyone – except ourselves when we get worried about them. Negative cyclic thinking, persistent and recurrent worrying or brooding.

**SSRI** – Selective serotonin reuptake inhibitors (SSRI's) are a class of antidepressant for treating depression, anxiety disorders, obsessive compulsive disorder and some personality disorders. These drugs are designed to elevate the level of the neurotransmitter serotonin.

**TRICYCLIC** – Tricyclic antidepressants are used to treat depression. They are also used to treat some other conditions such as migraine, panic disorder, obsessive compulsive disorder, recurrent headaches and some forms of pain. The word *tricyclic* refers to the chemical structure of the drug.

# SUGGESTED READING

**OVERCOMING OBSESSIVE COMPULSIVE DISORDER**
A self-help guide using Cognitive Behavioural Techniques
By Dr David Veale & Rob Wilson
Robinson

**WHEN ONCE IS NOT ENOUGH**
Help for Obsessive Compulsives
By Gail Steketee & Kerrin White
New Harbinger Publications Inc.

**OBSESSIVE COMPULISVE DISORDER: THE FACTS**
By Padmal De Silva & Stanley Rachman
Oxford University Press

**THE OCD WORKBOOK**
Your Guide to Breaking Free from Obsessive Compulsive Disorder
Aimed at sufferers embarking on a self-help programme
By Bruce M Hyman and Cherry Pedrick
New Harbinger Publications Inc

**BRAIN LOCK**
Free yourself from Obsessive Compulsive Disorder
By Jeffrey M Schwartz
Harper Collins

# THE IMP OF THE MIND
Help in coping with 'bad' thoughts
By Lee Baer
Plume, USA

# INVALUABLE ORGANISATIONS

**OCD ACTION**
Aberdeen Centre
22-24 Highbury Grove
London
N5 2EA

Help and Information Line: 020 7226 4000
Office: 020 7226 4545
Email: info@ocdaction.org.uk
Website: www.ocdaction.org.uk

**OCD-UK**
PO Box 8115
Nottingham
NG7 1YT
Telephone: 0870 126 9506
Email: admin@ocduk.org
www.ocduk.org

# SUPPORT GROUPS

The Priory North London
First Sunday every month from 7pm to 9pm
For over 16's
OCD sufferers and family members/friends
welcomed
For further information contact
alisonislin@btconnect.com

Edgware OCD Support Group
BIRU, Edgware Community Hospital, Burnt Oak
Broadway, Edgware, HA8 0AD (entrance via
Deansbrook Road)
Second Tuesday every month from 7.30pm to 9pm
OCD sufferers and family members/friends
welcomed
For further information contact the OCD Action
office: 020 7226 4000
Email: edgwareocd@yahoo.co.uk

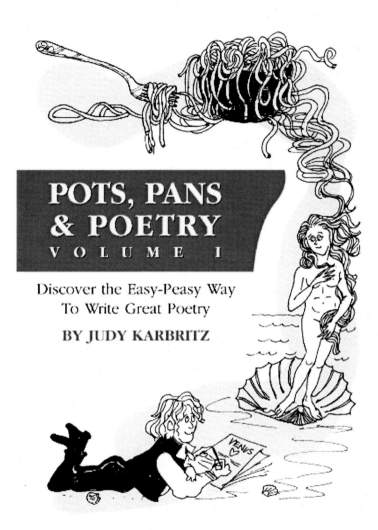

# POTS, PANS & POETRY
## V O L U M E  I

Discover the Easy-Peasy Way
To Write Great Poetry

BY JUDY KARBRITZ

Also published by Poetry Press Ltd
(www.potspandpoetry.co.uk)